abcdefgni

jklmnopqr

stuvwxyz

THE SESAME STREET BOOK OF LETTERS

created in cooperation with
the Children's Television Workshop,
producers of Sesame Street.

A Preschool Press book distributed in
association with TIME-LIFE BOOKS,
Little, Brown & Co., and
General Learning Corporation.

New York

> **PLEASE...**
> consult the last pages for
> suggestions about how best
> to work with this book.

The Sesame Street Book of Letters was editorially developed by
The Preschool Press of Weiner Communications Systems, Inc.,
Eleanor B. Feltser, editor.

Charles I. Miller and James J. Harvin, designers.

The Sesame Street Book of Letters was developed from material
provided to the Sesame Street series of Children's Television
Workshop by the following film companies:
Ken Snyder Enterprises, Los Angeles
Imagination, Inc., San Francisco
Tee Collins, New York City

Book trade distribution by Little, Brown & Co., Boston.

THE SESAME STREET BOOK OF LETTERS

A is for apple and also for ant
who tries to climb up it
but finds that he can't.

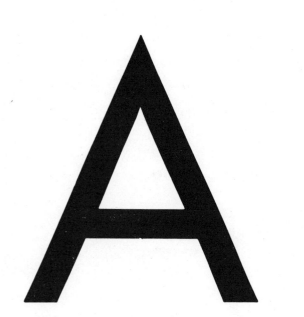

ABCDEFGHIJKLMN

A happy hole holds a heap of high humor.

H

OPQRSTUVWXYZ

Six silly sailors came sliding down our street.

S

ABCDEFGHIJKLMN

Unzip the zipper on a zany balloon and zoom! You've got zero.

Z

OPQRSTUVWXYZ

After his X-ray, Max mixed a fox and an ox in the box.

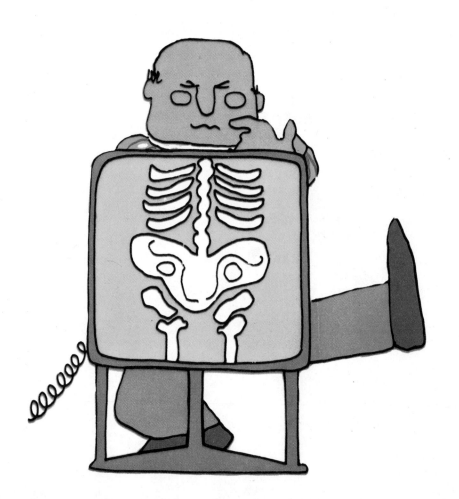

ABCDEFGHIJKLMN

Does this key open a mystery door
to a kennel, a kitchen or a king on the floor?

OPQRSTUVWXYZ

Yesterday's yellow yo-yo can make you yawn today.

Y

ABCDEFGHIJKLMN

X K Y

OPQRSTUVWXYZ

Only open doors in oily old balloons

ABCDEFGHIJKLMN

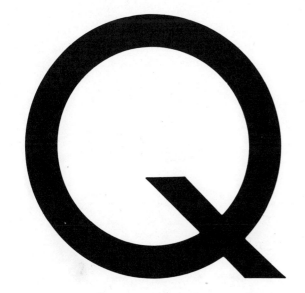

Quick as a quiver, quarters drop quite quietly into the quarrelsome pig.

OPQRSTUVWXYZ

If your cat catches a cold,
give him a candy-coated cod-fish.

C

ABCDEFGHIJKLMN

Great grumpy goats gallop through gates to gobble up green grass.

OPQRSTUVWXYZ

C

G

OPQRSTUVWXYZ

I've got an idea that Ida and Irene like icy ice cream.

I

ABCDEFGHIJKLMN

Trains that are tardy must try to make time.

OPQRSTUVWXYZ

Don't leave your ladder leaning long against a tall wall.

ABCDEFGHIJKLMN

Joe saw a junebug on his toe.
Put it in a jar and started to go.

J

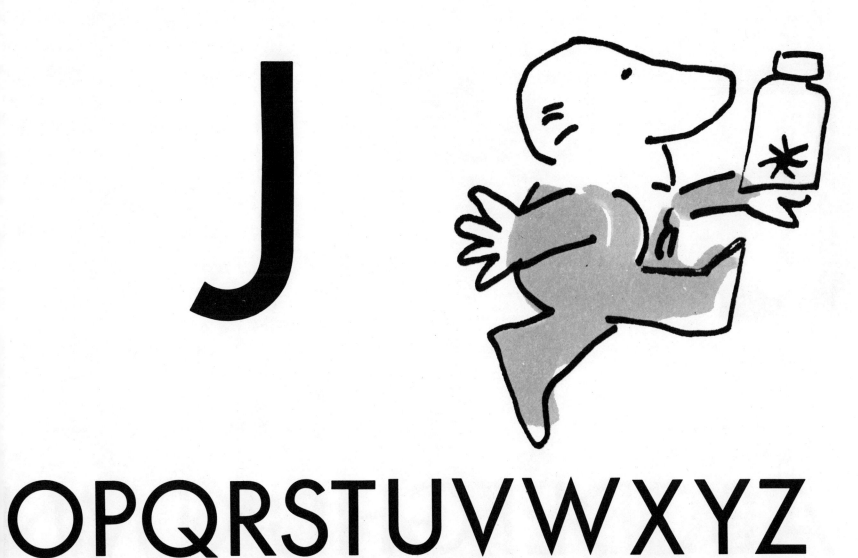

OPQRSTUVWXYZ

Eastern elephants who eat E's have easy meals.

E

ABCDEFGHIJKLMN

**F is for frog, and for fly and for fish,
sitting together each making a wish.**

F

OPQRSTUVWXYZ

I T L

ABCDEFGHIJKLMN

J E F

OPQRSTUVWXYZ

**If you dig a dinosaur,
drop your duck for a dime.**

D

ABCDEFGHIJKLMN

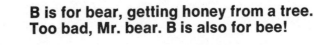

**B is for bear, getting honey from a tree.
Too bad, Mr. bear. B is also for bee!**

B

OPQRSTUVWXYZ

Pirates wearing patched paper pants in the palace are peculiar.

P

ABCDEFGHIJKLMN

**R is for rooster and rowboat and rain
that causes the robber to go down the drain.**

R

OPQRSTUVWXYZ

D   B

ABCDEFGHIJKLMN

P

R

OPQRSTUVWXYZ

M

Little mice love making mud pies
but their mammas don't. Oh my!

ABCDEFGHIJKLMN

Witches who wash their wigs on windy, winter Wednesdays are wacky.

W

OPQRSTUVWXYZ

Norman is nutty to notch a balloon with a nail.

ABCDEFGHIJKLMN

Old Lady Upton, underneath an umbrella
went floating on upwards, like a regular fella.

U

OPQRSTUVWXYZ

Violinists who vex visitors with violent vibrations should be vetoed.

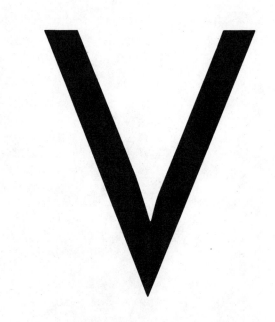

ABCDEFGHIJKLMN

M

L

ABCDEFGHIJKLMN

D K R

OPQRSTUVWXYZ

P

W

ABCDEFGHIJKLMN

B T F

OPQRSTUVWXYZ

o

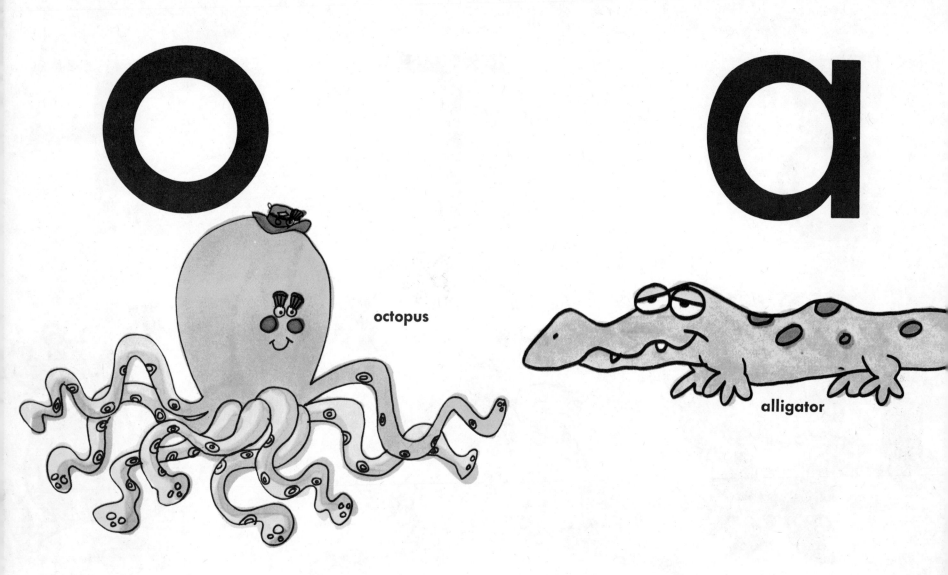

octopus

a

alligator

abcdefghijklmn

c

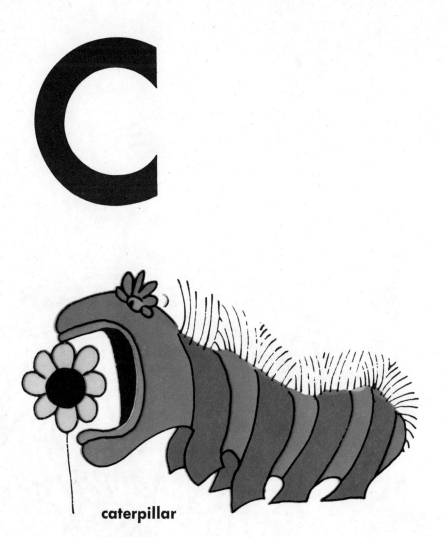

caterpillar

e

egg

opqrstuvwxyz

butterfly

dog

abcdefghijklmn

q

queen

a b c d e f g h i j k l m n

b  d g

p

pin

q

opqrstuvwxyz

i

ice cream

j

jam

abcdefghijklmn

f

t

fly

tiger

opqrstuvwxyz

l

lunchbox

r

radio

abcdefghijklmn

i  j f

t l r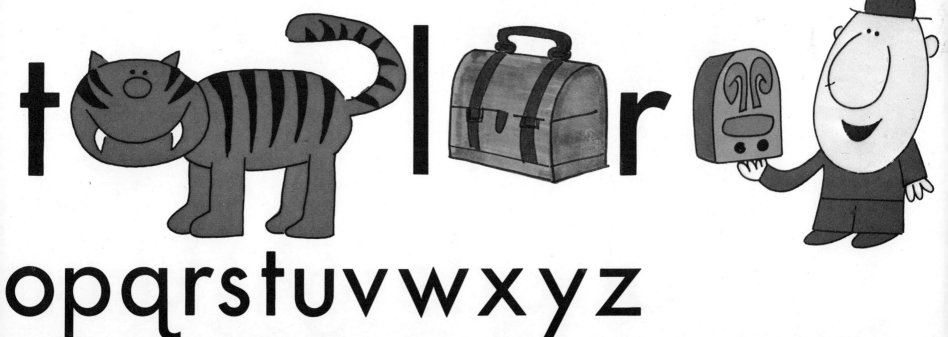

opqrstuvwxyz

m

w

mailbox

MAIL

walrus

abcdefghijklmn

n h

nest

horseshoe

opqrstuvwxyz

U

under

y

yawn

abcdefghijklmn

m w n

MAIL

h u y

opqrstuvwxyz

X

X marks the spot

v

viking

k

kitten

abcdefghijklmn

S

snake

Z

zebra

opqrstuvwxyz

g

h

abcdefghijklmn

j n v

opqrstuvwxyz

A NOTE TO ADULTS

On these pages, we have suggested ways to use the material in this book to greatest advantage to help your child learn. But helping your child build confidence is more important than any of the specific suggestions.

A child learning to walk needs more than sheer muscle development, to be successful. He also needs to develop confidence that he *can* walk, and he needs to feel that there is a good reason for walking. A child learning something new needs to gain that same confidence and motivation about learning.

How do you help him gain these things? By being ingenious and patient and, above all, friendly. When you're with him, give him your full attention. Follow his lead, and let his questions direct you. When he figures something out, be as excited as he is. And if it takes him a little longer with some ideas, stay relaxed. Remember, he's got many months to explore these pages. For now, it's the process of learning that's important, more than any particular information. And as long as he's enthusiastic, he'll be absorbing knowledge.

YOU'RE A LANGUAGE TEACHER!

You're about to help your pre-school child discover a totally new approach to language. It's called the written alphabet. To your child, it consists of a lot of squiggly lines that he's seen before in books and television. It seems to have something to do with the words people speak, but just how is probably still a big mystery. He's undoubtedly curious about how it works, but he has to absorb a lot of information before it will begin to make any sense to him.

WHY NOT A TO Z?

The first thing you have probably noticed about this book is that the alphabet is not arranged in the normal order. There is, of course, a reason for this. Consider again that your child sees squiggles instead of alphabet letters. Many of the squiggles seem very similar to each other. To your child's untrained eye, they may seem identical, especially since he has no particular reason to remember the differences. As yet, they have no meaning for him. One of the first things he needs to discover is how to distinguish between the squiggles—*to recognize the individual shapes.*

NAMING THE SHAPES

To make it easier for him to see the differences, similar shapes have been put close together into 'shape families'. Each member of a family uses the same basic shape in some way: O, C, Q, and G, for instance, are all variations on a circle, D, B, P, and R are all 'half-circle and straight line' combinations, and so on. After the introduction of each family, there is a concise review. As you turn to each letter, have your child trace the letter with his finger. See if he can discover the difference between the shapes on facing pages. Of course, at first you will be supplying *the name for each letter*—i.e., 'dee' for 'D' See if he can tell you the names of the letters as he comes across them. After all, he's trying to put the shapes and names together, so he might as well get as much practice as possible.

THE SEQUENTIAL ALPHABET

We have included the alphabet in normal, sequential order on almost every page. There are several ideas your child can discover with this. For one thing, he can learn that *letters are parts of the alphabet.* This is not so self-evident as it might seem, especially at first, when the shapes are still strange. You can help him see the relationships. Ask him to find the letter featured on each page in the alphabet at the bottom. This can be hard for a small child to do at first. There are so many interesting shapes, it's easy for him to forget what he's looking for. But it you help him, and if you are friendly and patient, after a while he'll get the hang of it. You might help by decreasing his choices at first, pointing to the right letter and one other, and asking him which is 'it'.

Another thing he can learn from exploring the full alphabet is that *the alphabet itself is not unlimited.* Think of it from your child's point of view. To him, it may seem that these strange squiggles just keep on coming. It's reassuring to know that there is an end in sight. Point out to him that there are only 26 letters, each with two forms—the capital and the small letter. Once he's learned them, he's learned all the alphabet there is.

And there is a final point. Eventually your child will need to know the alphabet in its normal order. It's not really important that he learn it right now, but it's there for whenever you feel the time is right.

You have probably noticed that the book has been divided into two sections: one for capital letters, and another for small letters. This ensures that your child will deal with letter shapes that look like the one he's trying to find. The capital and small letters have also been separated because they do not fall into the same shape families. If you feel that your child could benefit from seeing the two combined, please turn to the endpapers of the book.

THE JINGLES

The jingles are there for your child to enjoy. Perhaps he will like the sense, or nonsense. Maybe the rhythm or sound of the words appeals to him. He may have heard one while watching *Sesame Street.* He may dislike a particular jingle. If that's the case, help him make up his own jingle, using words that start with the letter on the page.

While he's enjoying the jingle, you can slip in some information. You can point out the individual words in the jingle and help him discover that *words are made up of letters*—not stars or squares or numbers or anything else. At the same time, you can help him understand that *letters represent sounds.* Point to words that start with the same initial letter, and say the words for him. See if he can tell you what the sound of the initial letter is, before you tell him.

THE MATCHING GAME

Following each alphabet section, there is a matching game section. The idea, of course, is for your child to match the letters with the picture of an object whose name starts with the letter. Since we have not covered all the letters in this section, you might want to enlarge it. One way to do this is to have your child collect pictures from newspapers and magazines and try to match them with initial letter sounds. Or you may try the game with familiar objects around your home, or with your child's name and the names of his friends.

TO SUM IT UP...

The material in this book has been carefully arranged to provide a maximum of information for your child. It's up to you to provide the maximum of enjoyment while he discovers all the things the book can offer. Those discoveries will probably take him several months, so you can afford to take it slowly. There is lots of time, and lots of his own curiosity, working on his side. Concentrate on keeping it light and fun and pleasant for both of you.

This book is based on material prepared for the television series *Sesame Street,* produced by the Children's Television Workshop of National Educational Television. With funds from Carnegie Corporation, Corporation for Public Broadcasting, The Ford Foundation, Project Head Start, Markel Foundation, and the U.S. Office of Education, the Workshop's staff has carefully and continually child-tested their broadcast material to ensure that the content and presentation are geared directly to the tastes of three to six year old children. In developing the broadcast material, the Workshop has called upon the talents and experience of many leading researchers and educators in the area of early childhood learning.

If *Sesame Street* is available in your area, your child may have seen many of the elements in this book on the program. He might enjoy using this book in conjunction with the show. However, it is not necessary to watch *Sesame Street* to be able to use this book successfully. It has been designed and created for independent use in all parts of the country.

ABCDEFG
HIJKLMN
OPQRST
UVWXYZ